AVALOK

Adversology

Unconstitutional Stories

First published by avalok arts 2026

Cover design by avalok

First edition

ISBN: 978-93-5626-859-3

Contents

Dedication

To

Fraternity
of
Humanity

Epigraph

"A poet's work is to name the unnamable,
to point at frauds, to take sides,
start arguments, shape the world,
and stop it from going to sleep."
— Salman Rushdie

Preface

He was a weary witness.
   Tired and exhausted.
   It was too much
   of a load to carry.

Then

Every night he sat down
   and wrote poetry.

Now

I carry his book
   in my hip pocket.
   I am following his map
   Not yet weary,
   but a witness.

Unconstitution

WE, THE PEOPLE OF ___________, having solemnly resolved to unconstitute _________ into an UNSOVEREIGN UNSOCIALIST UNSECULAR UNDEMOCRATIC REPUBLIC and to unsecure to all its citizens:

INJUSTICE, social, economic and political;

UNLIBERTY of thought, expression, belief, faith and worship;

INEQUALITY of status and of opportunity;

and to promote among them all
UNFRATERNITY assuring the indignity of the individual and the disunity and disintegrity of the Nation;

IN OUR UNCONSTITUENT ASSEMBLY this _______ day of (Month), 20___, do HEREBY ADOPT, ENACT AND GIVE TO OURSELVES THIS UNCONSTITUTION.

Chisel chisel away

Chisel, chisel, away
  Night and day
  Let no one stop you
  Let that emerge what's true!

INJUSTICE

Injustice
Unliberty

Free Palestine

I went to the city square
  I held a placard

Which said 'Free Palestine'

Now, I've been put in a jail
  But they forgot something
  The placard is still being held outside

Which said 'Free Palestine'

Blown!

I was writing a poem
on children of Gaza
A missile hit
and blew my poem to bits

I serve my people

I am an MP
 A V. I. P.
 I serve my people

She came to my home
 Fell at my feet,
 she was crying.

I asked her 'Behen,
 What's wrong?
 Why are you crying?'

'My husband comes home drunk,
 Beats me up every day.
 Sirji, save my family,
 Talk to him.' She wailed.

Elections were coming.

She is a Voter.

I tenderly hugged her
 It felt good.

Told her I will help her.
  Sent her home.

I knew her husband
  He is my voter too
  He is the village head

I called him over
  I asked him
  why his wife is
  creating trouble.

He fell at my feet too.

Then, Village head
  slipped me a bundle.

Elections were near.

He said - Saheb, you know me, always loyal.
  Please try and handle my wife.

Elections are close. '

I understood, it is my responsibility to serve my people.

Next evening, I called the wife over.
  Told her I will help her.

She was dressed in silk sari.
  Was looking beautiful.

I gave her a drink.

Took her to my bedroom.

Camera men were ready.

I had my way with her.
Sent her home in an auto - rickshaw.

Later,

I shared the video with her
and her husband too.

I won the election.

I am an MP
A V. I. P.
I serve my people.

Weight of a vote

If weight of a vote
Is 5 kgs of ration
What is the weight
of freedom?

Just Safe

I lived in this house
  with my family for decades
  I have the papers to prove it.

Then a riot happened
  in my town.

I was away attending a wedding.

I returned to find the
  Government had bulldozed
  my home
  including my cobbler shack.

My papers are very safe in my bank.

Thank God for small mercies.

Bulldazed!

Freed Verse

I write poetry in jail
  Waiting forever for bail
  How long can I continue
  writhing? I do not know

It is difficult to keep penning
  poems about freedom and hope
  from the confines of my cell
  when you witness justice fail

Of late, my poems began
  writing themselves.
  My pen races across the page.
  It was writing free verse.

I was glad.
  At last, freedom had
  entered my cell.

U K

Power of my Vote

I am a poor villager
I had a vote

Leaders always tell us
The vote you have
is very powerful

This is your democratic right
To elect or remove your leader
Never forget

I stored my Voting card
In a very secure place
My vote was powerful

Elections were on
Canvassing began
Candidates folded their
Hands humbly
and asked for my vote

I felt powerful
I had a vote

Then

My landlord sent for me
 Asked about repaying the loan
 I showed my Voting card
 He let me go

He won the election

My vote really was powerful.

Bitter Half

I am a woman
I am married
have 2 children
My husband is a laborer

He toils day long
Is paid very little
He gives me half
Drinks the rest

I save half of the cash
In 1000 - rupee notes
For my children's education
Rest to feed my family

Then came the 8 PM broadcast
My half became useless
My husband found out
He took my savings

Went to the bank
Exchanged the half
Never came back

He was found dead.

Was

I was
  a little girl
  Was
  I just was

Then

My grandpa
  touched me

So did my uncle
  I thought it was love

Then they entered me

I knew something
  wasn't right

Now

I wasn't

Caterpillar and the rose

I nurture a flower garden on my little terrace
I love tending them.
The other day I spotted couple of caterpillars creeping,
consuming leaves and buds, eating.
Who should I save?
The worms or the roses?

Dharma Sankat!

Khoon ka Rishta – (Blood Relation)

They smashed my child's head on a rock
He lay dead but skull was bleeding

They ripped my clothes
and mounted me, drooling

My child's blood was flowing towards me
They did what they wanted to do with my body

I too started bleeding and
My child's blood mingled with mine

Is this Dharma?

B B

Family Man

I had a family

Things were not going well
  for our community

Over the years
  a kind of atmosphere was created
  in the nation to fear us
  Oddly this only added
  to our own insecurities

But I had my family

I am no brave man
  I had a wife and kids to take care of
  and my old mother too

They were my family

So I changed my name
  Shaved my beard off
  Learnt the ways of the majority
  I dressed like them and

began worshiping like them

I loved my family

All went well till
a terrible riot happened in my town
It was fueled by hatred and distrust

I was afraid

I had a family

I was buying vegetables in the local market
A crowd with swords and lathis approached me
Screaming and shouting

They grabbed me
dropped my pants

Now I am buried

My family had me
no more!

Poor

You are laughing
at me because
I am a poet, poor

I cry for you
because you don't
know why a poet writes
Poor thing.

6 Feet

Six feet of rope, taut.
  Fan stopped, papers
  on the floor!

Stench

I usually keep to myself
Avoid getting involved in neighborhood affairs

My next-door neighbor
got married
The girl was very young and pretty
I used to watch them from my balcony
Living together happily

Months passed
Our walls were thin
So close
The sounds seeped through
I could hear the loud arguments
Not in content but in volume

I'd close my windows
hoping to shut out the sound
Try to go to sleep

Then one night my den
which normally
reeked of cigarette smoke

was overwhelmed by a stench
emanating from
my neighbor's house

Dowry!

Tweaking

A tweak here, a cut over there,
  a turn of phrase.
  Pull back and look again.
  Read it out loud, sounds good?
  You have a poem there

It Was All Arranged

It was all arranged

I was not so thrilled
  I was going to get married
  I wanted to study more
  Graduate and become a teacher

But my Appa would not listen
  He said

'You're getting old
  Relatives are talking behind my back
  They're saying there is a lack
  that you have
  That's why you're without a suitor'

I ran to Amma tried to persuade her
  to influence Appa
  to allow me to complete my college degree
  Nothing worked

They found a boy
  Paraded me in front of him and his family

Then they had talks with Appa
about this and that

It was all arranged

I was going to get married

I did get married as arranged

It was OK
for the first few months
My hubby worked in an IT company
Not much of a talker
Moody

Mom-in-law was the boss of the house
Her hubby was long dead and gone

Then the hints and nudges began
My hubby told me
about this and that they talked about
with my Appa
Asked me where is this and where is that

Mom-in-law joined the chorus

Then it grew louder and more accusatory
Shouting where is this and where is that

Appa did not respond
He said he had done all he could
He didn't know about this and that

IT WAS ALL ARRANGED

I wished I were not married

Then one day
  while I was cooking
  I heard something behind me

Before I could turn around
  I was burning

It was all arranged

No wasting

My teenage son
grabbed my hand
I looked at him,
He said
'Papa, buy me a phone'
I felt a twinge in my heart
I didn't have the money
and I told him so.
My son didn't come back from
college in the evening.

In the morning
I found him hanging from a tree, limp.
I lowered him gently to the ground.
Then I thought why waste the rope,
And hung myself!

Senbazuru!

Sadako
  She couldn't fold her 1000th crane
  'Cos she ran out of time.
  Senbazuru!

Written August 6, 2024 - Hiroshima Day

Fuse

Poetry, essentially
is a short circuit.
Blows your fuse!

UNFRATERNITY

Unfraternity
Inequality

Click

Communal riots were happening in my city
People were slaughtering each other
on an unimaginable scale
Setting poor hutments on fire
raping women
The cops were involved too

I was disturbed
Called my friend
a brilliant engineer
Expressed my concern
about the number of people being killed

He was calm and logical
He told me
'Think! We are in a big city
Consider the ratio
The deaths are just a small percentage
of the population of this city
It has to be cleaned up
Don't fret too much'

I was disappointed

A few days later
my friend called me up
His voice was shaking
He said
'Bhai do call somebody
help my family and me
The rioters have surrounded my area
We are in danger
Please call the cops'

I replied
'You're part of that small percentage
Don't fret too much
It has to be done'

Click!

Scary

Does poetry scare you?
Why?
That it is a coded language
which bypasses your walls
reaches your heart?

Blue Hawaii Chappals

I used to go to school barefoot
I had gotten used to it
The other boys and girls
wore nice shoes and colorful chappals

My Papa had a little shop
repaired their shoes
Momma worked
in Saheb's house as a sweeper

One evening Papa called me
Patted me on the head
Gave me a pair of
Blue Hawaii chappals

Oh it was so spongy and soft
I felt I was walking on clouds
I hugged my Papa
Momma smiled
looking at me dancing

in my Blue Hawaii chappals

The next day I went to school
 I didn't walk barefoot
 I floated wearing my
 Blue Hawaii chappals

The boys stared at me
 and the girls giggled
 Teacher aunty said
 boy I am happy for you

I too was happy

For my Blue Hawaii chappals

Lunch time
 Rupa — she was very pretty
 came to me
 and said I really like your
 Blue Hawaii chappals

The boys were watching
 As soon as Rupa went away
 They rushed at me
 Beat me up
 tore my shirt

Threw my Blue Hawaii chappals
 far into the lake
 next to our school

I ran home crying
 Without my

Blue Hawaii chappals!

The Poetic Path

All who are born are destined to die.
  The path you choose is entirely on you.

And there are those who walk,
  helpless, down the poetic path.

The Wheel of Dharma

It was a huge painting
  Three men holding up
  the wheel of Dharma

I was inspired

I painted it after watching
  Amar, Akbar & Anthony
  Called it Unity in Diversity

Amar in an orange kurta
  Akbar in green satin shirt
  Anthony in white suit

It was the Center piece
  in my art studio
  I was proud of my painting
  Refused to sell it

....

I was lounging in my sofa

Watching TV with
Amar, Akbar and Anthony
on the wall behind me

Breaking news was showing
Riots and killings somewhere
I got tired, switched off TV
went to sleep right there

...

Something woke me up
A spray on my face
I lit the night lamp
Went to the bathroom

Looked in the mirror
and to my horror
saw my face splattered
with blood.

...

I couldn't make sense of it
Maybe it was a dream within a dream
I went back to my studio
my sofa was stained with blood.

...

I looked up
My painting was there
With Amar, Akbar and Anthony dead.

The Wheel of Dharma
  Lay shattered on the ground!

The Enemy

The insecure tyrant
    Fears artists and poets

They paint the truth
    Poems show the mirror

Poetry is the enemy
    Art is dangerous

Poetry is a deed!

Indeed.

Wedding Horse

I am a wedding horse
  I am the best here in my town
  Because I am a white stallion

Grooms always prefer pure white horses
  I don't know why
  But I am not complaining

Because my master Bhola
  rakes in the moolah
  during the wedding season
  Therefore
  he feeds me with carrots and apples

Bhola had a son Ambu
  He adored me
  Whenever he returned from college
  He'd come to me first
  caress my silky mane
  and take me for a walk

I am straying

Well
Ambu got engaged
to a beautiful mare
oops
sorry

to an absolute beauty
who was as white as me
Ambu and her? Night and Day!

On the day of the wedding
I was decked up like never before
After all
Bhola owned me
The big day in Ambu's life
was about to take place

I will be the pure white stallion
to carry him to the wedding venue
I was so proud
It was an honour

I am a horse
not intelligent
not human
We were halfway to the wedding hall
the street was narrow
Then I could see in front of me
a sword wielding crowd

Of course
I couldn't see left or right
that's always been

The crowd rushed down the street towards me
  I thought
  'Why are they attacking me?'

One of the attackers swung his sword
  I reared in fear

When I landed
  I saw Ambu's bloody face
  lying on the ground
  looking at me

I was a white stallion

Now
  I am red!

Regardless

A poet is one,
who having written
the perceived truth,
doesn’t edit it
goes ahead
and shares
with the world.

Regardless!

I am a PhD

I did my PhD
in social sciences
The subject was close to my heart

I am a brilliant guy
It was in my genes
I researched thoroughly
Wrote an incisive thesis
Defended it eloquently
in front of distinguished professors

I aced it
Got my PhD

Now I am successful
Teach in a prestigious college

I have a loving family
A brilliant daughter
She takes after me

She has moved to the USA
She too got her PhD

Became a professor
Just like me

Everything was alright

Then

I got the news that
she'd gotten married to..

I can't tell you about it

I am disappointed
'cos I am a PhD

Cataract

He was my gardener
very old
He minded my plot
with tender care
Grew very many
types of flowers

He would come shuffling
and knock on my door
in the morning
I would prepare strong filter coffee
offer him a cup

He would water the flowers
Instruct me about what fertilizers to buy
He was very knowledgeable
about such things and more

But the thing was
his vision was impaired
Couldn't see clearly
His eyes matched his grey beard

CATARACT

He was too poor
  to afford treatment
  What little he earned
  he used it to get drunk

I set up an appointment
  with a doctor I knew
  Told my gardener about it
  I said the expenses will be borne by me

The next day he came
  accompanied by a young man
  Told me he was his nephew
  The gardener said
  the nephew will take him to the doctor
  I gave him some money for the transport
  and for the doctor's fees

I didn't see him for some time

Then he turned up one day
  and started sobbing
  Wiping his face with the tail of his turban

When asked he said the nephew
  abandoned him and ran away with the money
  He never reached the Doctor's clinic

I did not know what to say
  Tried to console him
  Gave him some more money
  Then he went away
  Never saw him again

Later

News reached me
  that he had drunk himself to death

Cataract!

Painting poetry

Painting is poetry with colors
Poetry is painting with words!

Big Rod

I am Louis Rodrigues
   Anglo- Indian.

Mom was a Tamilian
   Dad was a Portuguese Goan
   Strong and tall as a tree
   Dad was an Engine driver

People called me Big Rod
   I was 6 feet tall
   with a rounded paunch

For decades,
   in my Railway colony, in KGF
   I was the Santa Claus

Come Christmas, I donned
   my musty costume

There are no reindeers here in KGF

Rode on Tonga

Visited the families
Shouted 'Oho'
and handed over gifts,
from my gunny sack
to the kids of the colony.

...

That was long ago,
I have shrunk
My belly is gone
I can't stand straight

Still, when Christmas comes
I dress up and go out
But, the kids have gone

The colony exists no more.
I walk down empty streets
with sack full of gifts

I dump them on the roadside
Limp back home
Clink my glass of wine
with the bathroom mirror.

Merry Christmas!

Dance of Democracy

General elections were announced

Leaders emerged, gave fiery speeches
  About world's largest democracy
  And how each vote counts

I was a voter too

Undecided

Then my neighbor approached me

Asked me whom are you voting for

I named a candidate

He pulled me aside
  He said he is from another religion,
  can't you find any one else

I named a candidate from my religion
  My friend hissed at me
  He is not from our community

I named a candidate from my community
He said the candidate is from lower caste

I named a candidate from my own caste

My friend came close to me
Brother I am from your caste too
Why don't you vote for me

Still undecided

I never have participated
in the Dance of Democracy!

Gandhi

He was Gandhi
had large ears, near to being ugly
Was physically weak, wore a piece of khadi
He had a broken smile,
Walked around in chappals

What mattered was what he had inside.
An unbreakable will.
Steadfast and forthright.

Above all,
Adherence to truth
and non-violence.

He was Gandhi

Don’t just stand there

Don’t just stand there,
Do something.
Sit.
Like a Buddha!

Tryst with Destiny

Long years ago,
  we made a tryst with destiny,
  and now the time comes when we shall redeem our pledge,
  not wholly or in full measure,
  but very substantially.

- Pt. Jawaharlal Nehru

Constitution

WE, THE PEOPLE OF ____________, having solemnly resolved to constitute _________ into a SOVEREIGN SOCIALIST SECULAR DEMOCRATIC REPUBLIC and to secure to all its citizens:

JUSTICE, social, economic and political;

LIBERTY of thought, expression, belief, faith and worship;

EQUALITY of status and of opportunity;

and to promote among them all

FRATERNITY assuring the dignity of the individual and the unity and integrity of the Nation;

IN OUR CONSTITUENT ASSEMBLY this ________ day of (Month), 20___, do HEREBY ADOPT, ENACT AND GIVE TO OURSELVES THIS CONSTITUTION.

Author's note:

My debut book ***Versology*** had no commas
and no full stops.

I called it the Interrobanger style.
A rebellion against conservatism
and grammatical rigidification.

This book does not strictly enforce that style.
Some verses follow the rules.
Some verses breathe
without commas
and full stops.

I believe the white spaces
around the words
speak more clearly
than me.

About the Author

avalok
Artist Poet
Compassionate witness
Compulsive coddiwompler

Navigating life with purpose
Floating towards the unknown

Art is about stretching canvas inches to infinity
Fleeting moments into light years

Publisher

avalok arts

Bengaluru
India

www.ingramcontent.com/pod-product-compliance
Ingram Content Group UK Ltd.
Pitfield, Milton Keynes, MK11 3LW, UK
UKHW061307190726
13845UKWH00036B/1265

9 789356 268593